Supply Chain Management

Strategy, Operation & Planning for Logistics Management (Logistics, Supply Chain Management, Procurement)

By:
James Stevens

Published by Shepal Publishing
All Rights Reserved
Copyright 2016, New York

Table of Contents

Introduction 3

Chapter 1: The Supply Chain – What it is and how to understand it 4

Chapter 2: Supply Chain Drivers 8

Chapter 3: Networks and the Supply Chain 12

Chapter 4: Factors to Consider When Making Network Design Decisions 15

Chapter 5: Transportation In a Supply Chain 24

Conclusion 31

Introduction

Supply chain management is one of the most important things you can learn in business, and at the same time it is one of the most overlooked. There are hundreds if not thousands of companies out there that have failed because they did not understand the basics of supply chains, and therefore did not know how important it was to manage them properly.

As long as people have been able to trade in objects and products, business has been around, and more importantly, supply chains have been around. The fact that they are as business itself should not come as a surprise, however, it should be surprising that so many people tend to forget that without proper consideration to their supply chains, catering to their customer's needs becomes almost impossible.

In this book, you shall take a look at some of the different principles that make up supply chain management. You shall gain insight into this supposedly mysterious would, where things can change at the drop of a hat, and where things have changed significantly in the last few decades. You will learn a little about the logistics that are involved in supply chain management, and learn why they have become such an important part of the theory.

Chapter 1:
The Supply Chain – What it is and how to understand it

Before we even begin discussing supply chain management, it is important that you understand what a supply chain is, and the issues that you will need to take into account when you are designing, planning and operating a supply chain. This chapter will seek to clarify some of these issues, and help you to understand the importance of making the right decisions when it comes to your supply chain.

To begin with, what exactly IS a supply chain? A supply chain is made up of all the participants that are involved in ensuring that a customer receives what they desire, whether they are directly or indirectly involved in the request made. Many people here this definition and immediately picture the suppliers or manufacturers, retailers and wholesalers, and believe that the chain ends there. However, supply chains also include the transporters, warehouses that are used for storage, and even the end users themselves.

Every organization or company that is involved in the supply chain carries out the functions that are involved in fulfilling a customer request. These functions include, but are not restricted to, research and development of new products, marketing, distribution, customer service, finance, and general operations.

To give an example of a supply chain, imagine that you walk into a Target outlet to buy yourself shampoo. The supply chain will begin with you, the customer, and your request for shampoo. The chain will then move on to the Target outlet that you are in. Target stocks its shelves using supplies that have probably been bought from a finished-goods warehouse or a distributor, who probably deliver the goods using a third party transporter. The distributor or warehouse is receives ITS inventory from a manufacturer, for instance, Proctor and Gamble (P&G).

The P&G factory has the raw materials it needs delivered by a number of suppliers, who in turn may have received their inventory from lower-tier suppliers. For instance, the material used to package the shampoo may have come from the Pactiv Corporation, who received the materials to make the packaging from other suppliers.

From the example above, you can tell that a supply chain is dynamic, and requires a constant flow of information, resources and products between each link in the chain. In this case, the flow of information ends with Target, who supply pricing information to you, the consumer. Once you have transferred your money to Target, the outlet then relays POS (point-of-sales) data and restocking orders to the warehouse or distributor, who then restock the outlet in exchange for funds.

The warehouse or distributor also has their own pricing information, and this is relayed to the Target outlet, as well as any delivery schedules that the distributor may have. Information such as this is exchanged through the whole supply chain, and at every stage of the chain, money changes hands to ensure that the process continues smoothly.

When orders are made online, for example, should you want to buy an iPhone from the Apple Website, the supply chain is similar. It includes you, the customer, the Apple store website, the iPhone manufacturing plant, and all of Apples suppliers and their suppliers. All the information that you need to purchase the iPhone, including pricing, availability of the product and the range of iPhones is all on the website. Once you have chosen your preferred iPhone, your order information is recorded and your credit or debit card is charged. The information you submit when you are making your order is used all the way up the supply chain to help fulfill your needs.

Objective of a Supply Chain

The main objective of a supply chain is to ensure that the greatest value is generated. The value, also called the Supply Chain Surplus, is the difference between the value of the final product and the costs incurred by the chain itself while attempting to fulfill the customer's request, and is calculated as follows:

Customer Value – Costs incurred by supply chain = Supply Chain Surplus

The value of the product the consumer receives may change depending on the customer, and is directly affected by the amount of money the customer is willing to spend on the product. The difference between these two is called the Consumer Surplus. The rest of the Supple Chain Surplus becomes the Supply Chain Profitability, which is the difference between the money generated from the consumer and the money that is used in effecting the supply chain. The more profitable the Supply Chain is, the more successful it will be.

In most supply chains that make a profit, the relationship between the profits and the supply chain surplus is very evident. The success of the supply chain should therefore be calculated in terms of supply chain profitability rather than the profitability of one link in the chain. In fact, focusing on profits in just one link of the chain usually results in a drop in profits for the whole chain.

For that reason, the decisions that you make when designing and managing a supply chain directly affect the success of the chain. For instance, Target and Amazon are examples of corporations that have succeeded thanks to the exceptional design, planning and operation of their supply chains. Compare these to the failure of companies such as Webvan, which did not pay close attention to the design and planning of their supply chains. Other companies have failed because they have been slow to adapt their supply chains to the changing economic environment and customer expectations.

For example, the bookstore chain Borders was one of the largest distributors of books and Cds in the 1990's. They achieved this feat by opening up a chain of superstores that could stock over 100,000 titles. These titles were available at a cheaper rate because the company was able to realize higher inventory returns at a lower cost as compared to their smaller bookstores. However, the emergence and rapid growth of Amazon in the early 2000's threatened its business model, as the website could offer a much wider variety for a much cheaper price. Borders management could not reinvent their supply chain to compete with Amazon, and by 2009, the superstore chain had lost almost 50% in revenue, and was suffering losses of hundreds of millions of dollars per year.

Poor decisions are usually made because the people in the driver's seat do not understand how to improve their supply chain performance. In the next chapter you shall learn some of the things that drive a supply chain, and how to structure these drivers so that you may get the most out of your supply chain and increase your firm's financial performance.

Chapter 2:
Supply Chain Drivers

In the previous chapter, I mentioned the fact that the higher your supply chain surplus, the higher your supply chain profitability, and therefore, the more successful your supply chain will be. Improving your supply chain performance is not hard, and begins with understanding the different drivers of the supply chain. There are two main types of drivers, *Logistical Drivers* and *Cross Functional Drivers*. These drivers are: facilities, inventory, transportation, (the Logistical Drivers) information, sourcing and pricing (the Cross-functional Drivers).

Before we move any further, it is important that we define the drivers, and consider their impact on the supply chain.

1. **Facilities** – these are the physical locations in the supply chain where goods are either stored, manufactured, or engineered. Two major types of facilities exist, production sites and storage sites. The location, capacity and rigidity of each facility will have an incredible impact on the supply chains performance. For instance, 2009 saw Amazon increase the number of warehouses it owned in an effort to improve its operations and cut down customer waiting times, therefore increasing its responsiveness. The next year, in an effort to increase the effectiveness of its operations Blockbuster *reduced* the number of outlets it had, thereby *decreasing* its responsiveness. The reduction in facilities ultimately led to the bankruptcy and consequent acquisition of the company, whereas Amazon's increase in facilities ultimately led to the increased success of the company.

2. **Inventory** – inventory includes the raw materials, products in the process of manufacture, and the finished products within the supply chain. By altering inventory policies, you can radically affect your supply chain's effectiveness and responsiveness. For instance, if a company supplies industrial equipment, it may be in its best interest to maintain a high inventory level, as the inventory they hold will maintain its value for a long period. However, in the fashion industry, it is usually more beneficial if the company keeps as little inventory as possible, and increases the number of new products that they produce. This is because in this industry, inventory loses value rather quickly, and therefore a company could make significant losses if it tries to hold on to its inventory for a long period of time.

3. **Transportation** – this encompasses all the movement of inventory from one point to another in the supply chain. Transportation is one of the most versatile drivers, as it can consist of multiple routes and modes, each with its own unique qualities. The modes and routes of transport can greatly affect the effectiveness of a supply chain. For instance, if you were shipping materials across the globe, it may seem logical to use a company such as DHL to transport your goods, as they will be faster than some conventional methods. However, the high cost of doing business with such a company may make the supply chain less profitable and therefore less efficient. Companies such as Amazon have gotten round this problem by adjusting their prices to include the shipping costs, and by ensuring that they have multiple facilities close to their customers, reducing transport costs. This enables them to provide services such as same day shipping.

4. **Information** – this is the data and in-depth analysis of facilities, inventory, transportation, costs, prices and customers throughout the supply chain. Information is by far one of the most influential drivers when it comes to performance, as it affects all the other drives. Information garnered from the analysis of operations can be used to increase the efficiency and responsiveness of the supply chain, thereby making it more profitable.

5. **Sourcing** – this is the selection of the individuals or entities that will carry out particular tasks within the supply chain, including storage, manufacture, transportation and management of information. Sourcing is also a very important driver, as it ends up dictating what tasks the company will carry out, and the tasks that it shall outsource. Decisions made concerning sourcing will affect the whole supply chain, especially the effectiveness and responsiveness of the chain. For instance, many companies outsourced the manufacture of their products to China, making manufacture more efficient. However, responsiveness suffered in the long term due to the long distance that the goods had to travel once they had been manufactured. In an effort to increase responsiveness, many of these companies began flying their products into the country. However, this increases the cost of transportation, meaning that if there is poor planning, the company is likely not to realize the benefits of outsourcing manufacture to China.

6. **Pricing** – this is a very important driver, as it is what the company or organization will use to define how much it charges for the goods and services that it provides. Pricing affects the buyer, meaning that it

affects the overall performance of the supply chain. For instance, if a transportation company charges according to the lead time provided by its customers, there are those who will order goods early to help save money, and others that will order goods just before they need them because they love the responsiveness. It is obvious that changes in price may affect revenue collected directly, but the more subtle effect may be the change in cost as you go up the chain, depending on the impact the alteration in price affects the other drivers.

The definitions outlined above deliberately try to describe logistics and supply chain management. Supply chain management includes using logistical and cross-functional drivers to raise the supply chain surplus. Cross-functional drivers are now some of the most important drivers in the supply chain, and even though logistics are still a key part of the chain, supply chain management is slowly moving towards focusing on the three cross-functional drivers.

Despite this, it is important to remember that none of these drivers work on their own, but rather, they interact with each other to establish the performance of the supply chain. In a well-designed supply chain, it is important to understand this interaction, and to realize that some trade-offs will have to be made to enable you to achieve your desired level of responsiveness.

Chapter 3:
Networks and the Supply Chain

The design of networks in a supply chain is very important, as the networks that are created within a supply chain will ultimately affect the supply chain profitability. For this reason, network design decisions are also very important, as they will directly affect the supply chain setup. Supply chain network design decisions involve various things, including assigning roles to different facilities, choosing the right location for manufacturing, storage and transportation related facilities, determining the capacity of each facility, and determining what markets each facility will cater to. These design decisions can be further categorized as follows:

1. **Facility role:** This is the role each facility should play i.e. selecting the processes that each facility will carry out

2. **Facility location:** This is the selection of suitable locales for your facilities

3. **Allocation of Capacity:** This is the capacity that should be allotted to each facility

4. **Market and supply allocation:** This is where you choose what markets each facility should serve, and what sources should be used to feed each facility.

All the decisions that are made while designing a supply chain network will affect one another, and it is important to take this into account when making said decisions. The decisions affecting the role of the facility are important because they dictate how flexible or rigid the supply chain will be. For instance, Nissan has plants all over the world to cater for each market that it serves. Before 1997, these plants served only the local markets that they were in. However, the Asian economic recession of the late 1990's hurt this business model, as the factories in Asia suffered from a lull in activity, while the demand in the rest of the world for Nissan automobiles and other products continued to increase. However, this demand could not be met by the local factories due to the structure of their networks, and the Asian factories could not help to serve the markets with excess demand. Changes in structure within the Nissan supply chain made it easier for local factories to deal with external markets, and help the automobile manufacturer deal with the constantly changing global market conditions.

This flexibility to respond to global market conditions has not only benefitted Nissan, but other Japanese manufacturers as well. For instance, Honda opened a number of plants in the US that allow them to assemble both SUVs and small cars on the same floor. When the global recession hit in 2008, this proved to be to Honda's advantage, as the demand for SUVs dropped considerably, but the demand for small cars did not, meaning that Honda made minimal losses compared to some of its competitors.

The location of your facility is also important because packing up and moving is a time consuming, expensive endeavor. A prime location can help to keep a supply chain profitable by helping to keep the costs low while still increasing the responsivity of the company. For instance, the first Toyota plant was built in Lexington, Kentucky in the late 80's, and ever since then they have continued to expand their presence on the continental United States. These plants have proven to be very profitable for the Japanese automaker, especially when the value of the Yen rose and cars produced in Japan became too expensive to compete with cars produced in the US. The local plants allowed the car maker to respond to the American market quickly without having to increase the costs of their supply chain.

Chapter 4:
Factors to Consider When Making Network Design Decisions

When making network design decisions, there are a wide variety of factors that need to be considered before settling on a final decision.

1. **Strategic Factors**

A company's competitive strategy will have a huge effect on the network design decisions that are made within the supply chain. Organizations that concentrate of cost leadership will lean towards finding low cost locations such as China and Indonesia to build their manufacturing plants, even if it means building the plants thousands of miles away from the target market. However, companies that are bent on being responsive will have factories that are closer to their target market, and may actually select areas that cost considerably more just so that they are able to react faster to their markets wants and needs.

Sometimes companies combine both these strategies so that they can appeal to a wider market. For instance, the Spanish clothing manufacturer Zara has production facilities in both Europe and Asia. Its plants in produce mainly generic, low cost clothing that will sell in bulk. However, its European outfits all produce more innovative, high cost designs whose demand fluctuates. These European plants are more responsive to the customer's needs, allowing Zara to create apparel that is targeted for the consumers tastes quickly, at a lower cost. By combining the two strategies, Zara is able to produce a wider variety of clothes than most of its competitors in a more profitable manner.

2. **Technological Factors**

The availability of different technologies will drastically affect network design decisions. For example, if a particular technology exhibits significant economies of scale, then it may just be simpler for the organization to have a few high-capacity locations, rather than multiple low-capacity locations. This is especially true in the manufacture of computer chips, which require large investments to build the factories that create them, yet they are relatively inexpensive to transport. For this reason, many semiconductor companies build very few high-capacity factories.

However, if the factories have low fixed costs, then it is better to open many local branches rather than one large plant. For instance, Pepsi and Coca Cola all have local lower capacity bottling plants in comparison to fewer, high capacity plants because bottling plants do not have a very high fixed cost. This allows them to have local bottling plants around the world.

3. **Macroeconomic Factors**

These include tariffs, taxes, transportation costs and exchange rates that are not tied to an individual company. As global trade increases, macroeconomic factors have begun to have a larger influence on the success or failure of supply chain networks. Because of this, it is important that companies remember these factors when they are making their network design decisions.

    (i)   **Tariffs** – Tariffs are the monies that must be paid when products and/or equipment is moved across a particular boundary, be it a city, state, or international boundary. Tariffs will have a very large impact on the location that a company decides to choose. For instance, if a particular area charges high tariffs, then organizations are either not going to supply that particular market OR they will set up local branches to ensure that they minimize what they pay in duties. Usually, higher tariffs will lead to a larger number of production locations within the supply chain network, with every location having a diminished allocation capacity. Tariffs have decreased worldwide with the help of organizations like the WTO and agreements such as NAFTA, the EU, and MERCOSUR. This has allowed global organizations to combine their production and distribution facilities.

(ii) **Tax Incentives** – These are reductions in tariffs and/or taxes that governments give to help stimulate their economies by enticing corporations to build their facilities in particular areas. Many governments give different incentives depending on the cities or towns that the corporations would like to relocate to, to further entice the companies to set up shop in those areas. For instance, BMW's US facility is in Spartanburg, South Carolina purely because of the tax incentives that are provided by the state.

Many developing countries create free trade zones, where tariffs are relaxed as long as the material produced is used for export. This gives corporations a strong incentive to set up plants in these countries so that they can exploit the low labor costs. One of the best examples of a government setting up a free trade zone is China, which set up a free trade zone near Guangzhou to attract organizations to the area in the early 90s.

Other tax incentives are usually given when organizations that are entering the free trade zones promise to offer certain facilities to the local workers such as training, food, and transportation. Sometimes the organizations offerings may be technological. For instance, China waived all tariffs on 'high-tech' products in an effort to get companies to bring in their state-of-the-art technologies.

There are states that also place minimum requirements on local content, and also limit imports to their borders to help develop local industries. These policies tend to force global conglomerates to set up local factories that are supplied by local businesses.

(iii) **Exchange Rate and Demand Risk** – Changes in exchange rates occur often. However, they can drastically affect the profits of a supply chain, especially one that supplies international markets. For example, between 2007 and 2010, the Japanese Yen strengthened considerably, and its value against the Dollar dropped by 43, from 124 in 2007, to 81 in 2010. This increase in the strength of the Yen meant that companies that had production in the country but shipped out to the US faced a number of problems. The main problem was that as production was paid for in Yen, but sales were made in Dollars, production costs in Dollars went up, while the returns in Dollars dropped, making it seem like production costs had risen, thereby decreasing overall profits. The same problem was faced by Japanese companies in the late 80s, which is one reason why many Japanese organizations built plants all over the world.

If you design your supply chain networks properly, you can take advantage of these changes in the exchange rate and increase your profits when they do happen. One of the best ways to achieve this is to ensure that there is some overcapacity in your network, thereby making the capacity flexible enough to be used in a variety of markets. This flexibility will allow your organization to alter production during these changes, letting you maximize your profits when the changes occur.

(iv) **Freight and Fuel Costs** – Changes in cargo and fuel costs have a big impact on the profits of a global supply chain. For instance, in 2010 alone, the cost of transporting raw materials such as fossil fuels and metals changed so drastically that within 3 months, the cost of transporting those materials fell by over 2,000 points. Such price fluctuations can be hard to deal with. The best course of action is usually to sign long-term contracts that are beneficial to your organization or by hedging prices on stock and commodity markets.

4. **Political Factors**

The political climate of a particular region, especially of developing countries, can play a major role in choosing a location. Organizations prefer to create installations stable countries where there are rules and regulations that have been well defined. Political risk is one of the hardest things to measure, however, there are some indicators that one could use such as the Global Political Risk Index (GPRI). This is a scale many organizations use when they are investigating promising new markets. The index tries to measure a country's capability to handle crises and shocks according to four categories: Government, Society, Security and Economy.

5. Infrastructure Factors

If you would like to set up a new facility in a new country, one of the most important things to look for is good infrastructure because poor infrastructure will eventually raise the costs of doing business. When China began giving tax incentives in the 1990s, many companies moved to Shanghai, Tianjin and Guangzhou, not because the labor was cheaper than anywhere else in the country, but because these areas had some of the best infrastructure in the nation. Infrastructure components that should be considered when designing a supply chain network include:

- Availability of sites and labor
- Transportation terminals such as railway stations, airports and seaports and their proximity to your site
- Road access and congestion
- Availability of utilities.

6. Competitive Factors

While designing a supply chain network, it is important to consider the size, strategy and location of the competition. One of the most basic decision all firms make is whether to place their facilities close to or far from their competition. The decision is ultimately decided when things such as availability of raw materials, access to labor, and the form of competition are taken into account.

 (i) **Positive Externalities** – these are situations where it makes more sense for competing firms to be close to one another because it benefits all of them. For example, competing retail outlets would rather be grouped together in a mall because the situation in the mall generates a higher demand.

Positive externalities take various other forms, such as when the presence of competing companies eventually leads to the improvement of infrastructure in a particular area. For instance, Japanese automaker Suzuki was the first foreign automaker to build a facility on the sub-continent. They created a local supplier network to help bring down costs, and their investment worked so well that Suzuki's competitors also built their facilities in the country, as they realized that it would be cheaper to manufacture their cars in the country rather than import them.

(ii) **Splitting the Market**

In some cases, there are no positive externalities and instead companies relocate to help garner a larger share of the market. Firms that compete in terms of distance from the customer rather than prices will tend to move closer together to split the market.

7. **Responsivity and Presence**

Companies that would like to have customers with short response times need to move closer to the said customers. For instance, convenience store owners or liquor store owners must be located close to their customer base, otherwise no one will come to their stores. However, large supermarket and hypermarket chains like Target and Wal-Mart have customers that are willing to travel a little farther to get what they want, therefore these organizations do not have to be as close to their customers as the convenience stores.

If a company is targeting customers that would like their purchases delivered, fast transportation will be key, especially if they are trying to supply same day delivery. However, the faster the transportation, the higher the transportation costs therefore it is important to consider creating a balance between distance and delivery time when considering the delivery business.

Companies like coffee shops need to be close to their customers for many reasons, chief of which is that they will be able to attract customers due to their proximity to work places or homes. Being close to their homes and workplaces can never be substituted by a faster mode of transport, as regardless of the speed of the vehicle, customers who are far away from the coffee shop will just not be attracted to it.

8. Logistics and Facility Costs

The last thing to consider would be the logistics and facility costs experienced within the supply chain. These change with the changes in number of facilities, locations, and allocation of capacities. Organizations should consider inventory, transportation and cost of the facilities when they are creating their supply chain networks.

Inventory and facility costs go up as more facilities are opened. On the other hand, transportation costs *DROP* as more facilities are opened. When there are so many facilities that the economies of scale are lost, then transportation costs will begin to increase.

Supply chain network design is also affected by the changes that happen at each facility. For instance, should there be a major drop in the weight or volume of raw materials as a result of processing, then it may be better to relocate the facility so that it is closer to the supplier, not the consumer.

Logistical costs are the sum of the stock, transportation, and facility costs. Facilities in a supply network should be enough to keep the logistical costs to a minimum. Companies could increase the number of facilities that they have past this point, especially if it is to improve response times to customers. However, the decision only makes sense if the company sees increased revenue from the improved response that helps to outweigh the increased costs of having more facilities.

Chapter 5:
Transportation In a Supply Chain

Transportation within a supply chain involves the movement of different products from one location to another until the final product reaches the consumer. It is very important in the supply chain as products are very rarely manufactured and consumed in the same area. Transportation is also one of the most significant components of the supply chain because it can be one of the most expensive drivers in the chain. In 2002, only housing, healthcare and food supplied a greater portion to the GDP of the US than transportation.

In global supply chains, transport plays an even bigger role. The success of companies such as IKEA has been built mainly on the effectiveness of their transportation networks. For instance, IKEA's sales for the financial year 2008/2009 came in at 21.5 billion Euros, mainly because its strategy is constructed around providing the best quality products it can at the lowest prices. One of IKEA's goals is to slash prices by at least 2% each year, and one of the only ways they can do this successfully is by sourcing local materials wherever they can, and ensuring that their worldwide transportation costs are as inexpensive as possible.

Another company that has found a way to reduce its transportation costs and therefore increase its supply chain profitability is Seven-Eleven Japan. The company's main aim is to ensure that the products it sells in its stores matches the customer's needs, regardless of geographic location and even time of day. They do this by ensuring that each Seven-Eleven receives several shipments a day so that the products on the shelves always match the needs of their consumers. Goods from different suppliers is collected on various trucks depending on various factors including temperature, to ensure that all the deliveries are made at the lowest cost to the company. This responsive transportation system, along with the compilation of goods from different suppliers, decreases the company's transportation costs considerably while guaranteeing that the products that are available to the customers meet their needs.

Many supply chains use responsive transportation to help streamline inventories and operate with fewer facilities. For instance, Amazon depends on different package carriers and the postal system to ensure that their customer's orders are delivered from their centralized warehouses.

In transportation, the *shipper* is the organization that needs the product to be moved from one place to another, while the *carrier* is the organization that actually moves the said product. For instance, when Amazon uses FedEx to transport customer's orders from the warehouse to the customer's door, Amazon is the shipper and FedEx is the carrier. Apart from the shipper and the carrier, there are two other parties that can affect transportation:

- The owners or operators of infrastructure like roads, ports, canals and airports
- The organizations that create the policies on transportation worldwide.

All four parties are responsible for the effectiveness of transportation.

To fully comprehend the effect of transportation in a supply chain, you need to consider the points of view of all four parties. Carriers invest in transportation equipment such as trucks, trains and ships, and in some cases the infrastructure as well, such as roads and rails. They then try and come up with ways to receive the most attractive returns on their investments. Conversely, shippers use transportation to minimize the total cost of their supply chains, while attempting to offer the best responsiveness to their clients.

However, this responsiveness is dictated by the quality of the infrastructure that the carriers are using. As most transport infrastructure is managed by public authorities, it is important that these authorities manage their funds wisely so that they can carry out maintenance and expansion when the time comes. The policies that are put in place by the different organizations that create said policies dictates the amount of resources that can be availed for improvement of transportation infrastructure. Many policies also aim to prevent the abuse of power by certain monopolies, while promoting fair competition and balancing environmental, social, and energy concerns in transportation.

Modes of Transportation

Supply chains use a number of different modes of transportation, mainly:

- Air
- Road
- Rail
- Water
- Pipelines
- Package carriers
- Intermodal

The efficiency of any mode of transport is dictated by the investments in equipment and operating decisions made by the carrier, as well as the infrastructure and different policies pertaining to transportation. The carriers main objective should be to make sure that they use their assets well while giving their customers the best service they can. The decisions made by carriers are usually affected by the cost of equipment, the cost of operating said equipment, the variable operating costs, the responsiveness the carrier is looking to provide, and the costs that the various target markets are willing to incur.

For instance, FedEx designed a hub-and-spoke airline network to help shorten deliver times, and make their deliveries more reliable. Conversely, UPS uses a combination of different modes of transport in an attempt to reduce the cost of delivery at the expense of delivery times. The major difference between the two companies lies in their pricing. FedEx charges are based on the size of the package that is being delivered, whereas UPS charges based on the size of the package AND its final destination. If you were to consider it from a supply chain point of view, it becomes obvious that the FedEx strategy is more appropriate when the cost of transportation is not affected by the destination of the package, and when delivery time is crucial. However, UPS's strategy is more appropriate when transportation costs are dependent on the final destination and the delivery time counts for less.

Air Carriers

Air carriers include both passenger and cargo airlines such as American, Southwest, United and Delta Airlines. Many of these airlines have three elements that dictate their costs:

- (i) Infrastructure and equipment
- (ii) Labor and fuel
- (iii) Variable costs that are usually linked to passengers or cargo carried.

Most of the cost that is encountered with air carriers comes during takeoff. This makes an airline's most important goal the maximization of income generated during each flight.

The best items suited for air transportation are small high-value items, emergency shipments, and other time sensitive shipments that need to travel large distances in short amounts of time.

Trucks

Significant portions of all the products that are transported globally are transported on trucks. Despite the fact that trucks are pricier than trains, they have the added advantage of being able to deliver door-to-door in a shorter time. Additionally, shippers do not have to worry about transfers between pickup and delivery.

Trucking has very low fixed costs in comparison to most other modes of transportation, and even one truck is enough for you to get into the transportation business. However, one of the biggest challenges with trucking is that most areas have an imbalance between imports and exports. For instance, New York imports a lot more than they export, meaning that truckers going to New York have to plan carefully to enable themselves to maximize revenue while minimizing empty travel time.

Rail

Rail carriers have some of the highest fixed costs, mainly because many of them have to invest in their own locomotives, rails, yards and cards. When considering the amount of idle time that trains have due to changing of cars and track congestion, the costs of owning a train can seem to skyrocket.

That is because even when the train is idle, fuel and labor costs are still incurred. These costs are considered to be more than 60% of the total expense of running the train. Therefore, to have a profitable operation, a train company has to keep its locomotives and crews on their toes.

However, they do face a myriad of different issues such as track and terminal delays, vehicle and staff scheduling, and terrible performance on-time. There is also a alot of time wasted during various transitions in the rail system. Another issue with the rail system these days is that unlike scheduled transportation, many trains are now 'built', i.e. they only leave the yard once enough cars have been coupled onto the locomotive.

For this reason, time sensitive packages, high-value, and short distance shipments rarely travel by rail. However, the pricing and load capability of the rail system makes it one of the best ways to transport large, heavy, and high-density products over long distances.

Water

There are many ocean carriers that operate globally today, including Maersk, Evergreen Group, American President Lines and the Hanjin Shipping Company. By nature, water transport is not available everywhere. In the US, water transport takes place along the inland water system which includes the great lakes and rivers like the Mississippi, and coastal areas.

Water is very well suited to carrying heavy loads at a low cost. However, being the slowest of all the modes of transport, it is unsuitable for use if you would like to deliver packages that need to be delivered quickly. However, it has been known to be effective as a short haul solution in the canals and rivers of Europe.

Despite the speed of water transportation, it holds the largest market share by far when it comes to transportation in global supply chains. For instance, over 70% of US imports and exports are made by ships. This is mainly because it is the cheapest option there is, especially when considering the weight carried and distance travelled per ship. The demand for shipping containers has been on the rise in recent years, and this has led to the construction of larger, faster ships. However, delays at ports, customs and security at ports means that there are still significant delays in the shipping industry.

Conclusion

The main objective of this book is to help you understand the basics of Supply Chain management, and some of the things that need to be considered when you are considering the practice. Many of the aspects of supply chain management that are outlined between these pages are just the tip of the iceberg, as the more time passes the more we learn about supply chain management.

For instance, a couple of decades ago, no one would have thought that global supply chains would be so common, and that there would be so many factors that could affect the supply chains. Before technology began to take over, very few states and countries had even thought of introducing tax incentives to help give them a technological advantage. Fast forward a few years and China became one of the first countries to do so aggressively.

Now, because of their understanding of the value of supply chain management, and the incentives that companies look for when they are looking to maximize profits, China is rapidly becoming an giant in all fields, including technology, construction and manufacture. The policies that countries like China and Singapore put in place to woo investors has seen their populations benefit because nations like these realized that by inserting themselves into major supply chains they could also benefit a great deal. Once you begin to understand supply chain management, you will begin to see just how much you can improve your current set up, and how you can maximize your supply chain surplus and therefore maximize your organization's profits.

Made in the USA
San Bernardino, CA
11 May 2017